# *Relapse Prevention*

---
## W O R K B O O K
---

## Judy Lohr

ISBN 978-1-64569-818-0 (paperback)
ISBN 978-1-64569-819-7 (digital)

Christian Faith Publishing, Inc.
832 Park Avenue
Meadville, PA 16335
www.christianfaithpublishing.com

Printed in the United States of America

# INTRODUCTION

—⚏—

This guide is for anyone who has stopped using alcohol or other drugs and wants to stay sober and drug free. Successful sobriety involves more than just the desire not to drink or use—it also involves hard work. Here you'll find the *tools* you need to begin.

This workbook is designed to help you stay sober. It is not meant to take the place of a twelve-step group, counseling, or an aftercare program. It is to be used in conjunction with them. The words "alcohol and other drugs" are used throughout this guide. For our purposes, your drug of choice doesn't matter. Whether you were addicted to cocaine, heroin, marijuana, alcohol, prescription drugs, or any other mind-altering chemical, the tools offered in this guide are meant to help you avoid relapse.

Whatever your particular situation is, you'll find it helpful to take your time with this guide. Pause and reflect on the material you have read. Think about the questions before writing your answers. Recovery can't be hurried—neither should this guide. In addition to proceeding at a relaxed pace, you'll find it helpful to include somebody in your work with this guide. It might be a sponsor, a counselor, or a close friend. You may wish to share and then discuss your work in each chapter before continuing further. This way you can ask questions, clarify what you've learned, and gain support for those difficult issues that might surface through your work in this guide. Your helper is also someone you can turn to if you were to relapse.

*The person I will ask to be my helper with this guide is:

_____.

# CHAPTER 1

—◠◡—

# Understanding Relapse

Simply put, a relapse is the return to drinking or using other drugs after a period of sobriety. Relapse more accurately describes a PROCESS rather than a simple drinking or using event. For some, this process is slow—twelve-step meetings are skipped, there is a return to old attitudes, and eventually the drinking or using begins again. For others, the relapse process is quick. They are feeling better than ever about themselves. They have every intention of staying sober. Then something happens and they end up drunk or high again.

It might be hard for some to understand how someone who has been enjoying the rewards of sobriety would be willing to return to despair and wreck relationships just for the sake of a drink or some other drug. As you know, perhaps from experience, it happens far too often.

The answer to this question is found in your recovery program and the everyday stresses of life. These stresses include both the little frustrations as well as the bigger problems. If you have a recovery program in place that can effectively deal with life's problems as they arise, you're not likely to relapse. It's when your recovery program isn't meeting your needs that the first cracks begin to appear in the foundation of sobriety. If you don't have the tools and the resources to deal with life's stresses, you'll begin to fall back on ways of coping that didn't work very well in the past such as avoidance, being passive, or blaming other people. Since you aren't solving these problems, they begin to pile up.

If you don't turn things around, you'll cut yourself off from your support system. As the pain increases, drinking or using other drugs will begin to look attractive. This comes as no surprise—it is how you previously dealt with problems in your life. Your sobriety now consists of nothing but sheer willpower, and you are going at it alone. The final phase of relapse, which is not far off, is drinking and using other drugs once again.

When people refer to "living clean and sober" or "being in recovery," they are talking about more than simple abstinence. True sobriety is not just a matter of refusing to drink or use other drugs—but learning how to live a full life without them. The good news is that it is possible to stop yourself at any time during a relapse progression—long before you use.

Using doesn't mean that you've blown your one chance at sobriety—it just means there are some additional tools you must add to your recovery program.

# CHAPTER 2

# Recognizing Dangerous Situations

As a recovering person, you'll occasionally find yourself in situations where you are thinking of drinking or using. These situations will be as diverse as each of you. The recovering community urges you to "avoid slippery people and slippery places!"

What some refer to as a *slip* is still a relapse. This term simply points out the difference between a long series of binges, broken promises, and tragedy (a full-blown relapse) and a single drinking or using episode from which you can learn. Though still both dangerous and upsetting, a slip can motivate you to look at why it happened and what you can do to make sure it doesn't happen again.

Before you can stay out of slippery places you must know where and what they are.

*Five situations that are dangerous for me:

1. _____
2. _____
3. _____
4. _____
5. _____

The simplest way to deal with your dangerous situations is to avoid them entirely. Read through your list and make an *X* through those situations you can avoid. For situations that you cannot avoid, make a plan. For example, decide how you'll answer questions concerning your beverage choices.

*Choose two of your dangerous situations that can't be avoided and make a coping plan:

Situation #1:
How I used to deal with it _____
How I will deal with it now _____

Situation #2:
How I used to deal with it _____
How I will deal with it now _____

# CHAPTER 3

## Identifying Relapse Warning Signs

As discussed earlier, relapses don't just happen. They have a beginning, middle, and end with signs along the way. These warning signs can be very helpful because if you heed them, you can turn back before you actually take that first drink or other drug.

*Place a check by any of these relapse warning signs that could apply to you.

_____ overly confident/cocky

_____ setting unrealistic goals

_____ rejecting advice

_____ constant boredom

_____ minimizing problems

_____ talk of "good old days"

_____ covering up feelings

_____ secret dissatisfaction

_____ dishonesty

_____ defensiveness/blaming

_____ people pleasing

_____ impatience

_____ loneliness/isolation

_____ not managing depression

_____ forgetting to be grateful

_____ difficulty sleeping

_____ reduced work/school effort

_____ complacency

_____ sporadic meeting attendance

_____ not calling sponsor

_____ preoccupation with drinking

_____ perfectionism

_____ not managing anger

_____ unwise use of time

*Additional relapse warning signs for you:

_____

_____

*From the group of warning signs you checked, circle the five most likely to show up in your life if you began moving toward relapse. Think of a plan to correct the problem.

1. Warning sign: _____
   I need to: _____

2. Warning sign: _____
   I need to: _____

3. Warning sign: _____
   I need to: _____

4. Warning sign: _____
   I need to: _____

5. Warning sign: _____
   I need to: _____

# CHAPTER 4

# Helping-Hand Contract

Sometimes you might not notice your own warning signs. You can ask for help from family, AA or NA members, your sponsor, your designated helper with this guide, a counselor, or other friends. They might notice something that concerns them but feel awkward about bringing it to your attention, wondering if it's really any of their business. Complete the following contract and then ask people who have regular contact with you and are aware of your commitment to sobriety to read and sign the contract.

It's possible for me to be headed toward a relapse without my realizing it. I value your opinion and need you to tell me if you have any concerns about my sobriety. Here is my list of warning signs indicating I might be heading toward alcohol or other drug use:

1. _____
2. _____
3. _____
4. _____
5. _____

If you notice any of these signs or see me getting into trouble in other ways, please tell me. Don't wait until it's too late. If you do point out a concern to me, I promise I will try to listen without becoming defensive because I know you care about me. If I don't listen to your concerns, or if my behavior doesn't improve, I want you to take these steps:

1. Contact my sponsor or counselor.
2. Insist I return to a treatment program.
3. Kick me out of the house.
4. _____.

**For family and friends to sign:**

If I notice these relapse warning signs, I will speak up and let you know of my concerns.

_____

_____

**For you to sign:**

I promise to listen to any concerns you might have and follow through with any recommendations.

Signed: _____

# CHAPTER 5

—⚬—

# Preparing for the
# Possibility of Relapse

I t would be wonderful if everybody who made a commitment to sobriety would never use again. Unfortunately, that's not the case. Some people return to drinking several more times before they establish a solid recovery program. There are those who never get a second chance at sobriety.

Though it surely won't be a happy time for you, all is not lost if you drink or use again. A great deal depends on what you do next. You can either get back up and carry on, or you can stay down and turn a slip into a full relapse. While it seems like a simple decision right now, you most likely have a clear head and a commitment to sobriety. That won't be the case when you wake up the morning after a night of drinking or using. The fuzzy thinking, the guilt, and the shame can motivate you to continue drinking or using.

What can you do to lessen the odds of a long binge? HONESTY. If you keep your relapse a secret, it probably won't be your last. Your support system should be told. You need the support these people can offer. You cannot successfully recover from a relapse by yourself.

You also need to be honest with yourself. Retrace your steps back to the initial stages of the relapse. All relapse episodes begin somewhere. Maybe you made poor choices; maybe you didn't have all the tools you need to stay sober. Once you have identified what went wrong, you can make the necessary changes.

*If I were to relapse, it would be important for me to tell these people:

_____

_____

_____

*If I were to relapse, here are the steps I should take to make certain it doesn't happen again:

_____

_____

_____

# CHAPTER 6

—ɯ—

# Dealing with Your Feelings

Uncomfortable feelings can trigger the start of a relapse. Actually, it isn't the uncomfortable feelings themselves, but the lack of knowing how to deal with them. As long as you are breathing, you'll experience a variety of different feelings—some uncomfortable, some pleasant. Now that you're not drinking, you need to develop different ways to cope with the many different feelings which will flow through your heart and mind. If you don't manage your feelings in healthy ways, they begin to pile up inside of you.

Where to start? If you don't clean house, this heavy ache will convince you to drink or use once again. As you learn how to deal with your uncomfortable feelings without using, they will begin to seem less troublesome. You will learn that feelings, like the weather, simply come and go. Here is a list of uncomfortable feelings that people experience:

| | | | |
|---|---|---|---|
| abandoned | disappointed | hurt | rejected |
| afraid | discouraged | inadequate | remorseful |
| aggressive | disgusted | insecure | resentful |
| angry | dissatisfied | irritable | sad |
| annoyed | enraged | jealous | tense |
| anxious | exasperated | lonely | terrified |
| bitter | frustrated | nervous | threatened |
| bored | guilty | paranoid | uneasy |

| concerned | helpless | perplexed | unloved |
|-----------|----------|-----------|---------|
| confused | hopeless | powerless | worried |
| desperate | hostile | regretful | worthless |

*List five feelings that are difficult for you to cope with:

1. _____  2. _____  3. _____
4. _____  5. _____

*Choose one feeling from your list of five which is especially difficult for you to deal with: _____

*What situations typically bring about the feeling you selected?

1. _____
2. _____

*What do you usually do to deal with this feeling?

1. _____
2. _____

Some methods of coping with feelings work better than others. If you try to avoid your feelings because they are painful, embarrassing, or scare you, then they will keep resurfacing again and again. You've listed ways you currently deal with a particular feeling. Now think of several better ways to cope with this feeling.

*Better ways to cope with this particular feeling.

1. _____
2. _____

*Choose another feeling from your list that is especially difficult for you to deal with: _____

*What situations typically bring about this particular feeling?

1. _____
2. _____

*List examples of what you do with this feeling.

1. _____
2. _____

*Describe better ways to cope with this particular feeling.

1. _____
2. _____

**Recovery Activity**

For one week, spend five minutes at the end of each day reflecting on the various feelings you experienced that day. Do you notice any patterns? (Journaling is a good way to keep track and chart your progress.)

# CHAPTER 7

# Building Relationships

Men and women with healthy recovery programs have discovered that they can't stay sober by themselves—they need others. A hallmark of chemical dependence is strained or destroyed relationships. Now that you have stopped using, it's time to both rebuild damaged relationships with family and friends and seek out additional, fulfilling connections. These relationships will not only help ease feelings of loneliness and alienation, but will also support you in your efforts to grow in recovery. Members of your twelve-step group can show you how to apply the twelve steps to your own life. Both nurturing and sustaining these friendships offer a solid foundation for your recovery.

*List the people in your life with whom you currently have nurturing relationships.

1. _____    2. _____
3. _____    4. _____

Beside each name, record how many hours you have spent together during the past month. What do these numbers tell you? It's difficult to get the support you need from a friend who lives far away or doesn't have free time. You need regular ongoing time with people you care about and who care about you. If you can't get what

18

you need from all four of these people, look around for additional opportunities.

*List people who you would like to get to know better.

1. _____     2. _____

The secret for getting new relationships off the ground is to make the first move. Being a member of a twelve-step group makes meeting people easy. Ask someone to join you for coffee after a meeting, attend your group's social functions, or arrive thirty minutes early to your meeting.

*For each of the people you listed above, identify the next step you can take to help build a relationship.

1. _____
2. _____

**Recovery Activity

Choose one of the people on your list and follow through with your next step.

# CHAPTER 8

—ⱲⱲ—

# Managing Your Stress

Stress is something you manage, not something you erase from your life. Not all stress is harmful. Small amounts of stress can be helpful by motivating you to finish a project for example. If you're not able to manage large amounts of stress, it's likely you'll slide back into old habits and ineffective ways of coping with problems.

*Which situations or problems are likely to produce stress for you?

1. _____    2. _____
3. _____    4. _____

There are many different ways to feel stress. It might show up in your body as a backache, a splitting headache, accelerated breathing and pulse rate, irritability, or sleeplessness.

*How do you know when you are stressed?

1. _____    2. _____
3. _____    4. _____

People react differently to stress and some of these actions relieve the stress while others can even increase the stress level. Some people avoid it and hope it will go away, scream into a pillow, take frustrations out on the family, develop an ulcer, or use some mind-altering drug.

*What do you currently do when you are feeling stressed?

1. _____     2. _____
3. _____     4. _____

*Here are some other suggestions:

1.  Write out a list of all the things you did accomplish today instead of worrying about what you didn't get done.
2.  Close your eyes and breathe deeply a number of times, slowly.
3.  Vividly imagine a peaceful, serene place.
4.  Listen to a relaxation tape or other soothing music.
5.  Go for a walk, meditate, take a short nap.
6.  Begin a regular physical activity such as bike riding.

*What are two new stress-reducing activities you can try?

1. _____     2. _____

**Recovery Activity**

Practice a new stress relieving activity.

# CHAPTER 9

# Learning How to Say No

"No thanks. No, really, my soda's just fine." Most people will respect your desire not to drink or use, but others seem to feel compelled to push it a little too far. It's a good idea to think about this probability in advance, before aggressive offers wear down your defenses and you find yourself holding a beer, a glass of wine, or a joint. It is common for newly recovering people to worry about what others think when they refuse a drink offer. Ultimately, you must live by your own values.

*List five situations or people who make it difficult for you to say no to alcohol or other drugs.

1. _____  2. _____
3. _____  4. _____
5. _____

*Now identify why it's difficult for you to say no in these situations or to these people.

1. _____
2. _____
3. _____

For each difficult situation or person you have listed, think of a positive and assertive way to take care of yourself. In some situations, you might find that all you need to do is say, "No thanks, I'm not drinking tonight." With others, you might need to state your needs more clearly: "No thanks. I don't drink anymore." There might be still other situations or people you just have to avoid altogether.

*List one positive way to handle each situation or person on your list.

1. _____     2. _____
3. _____     4. _____
5. _____

**\*\*Recovery Activity**

Make certain your close friends are aware of the fact that you no longer choose to drink or use other drugs by taking a few minutes to explain this to them.

# CHAPTER 10

─── catch───

# Overcoming Urges to Use

Occasionally, even when you are taking care of yourself and doing everything right, you might get an impulse to drink or use other drugs. These urges can be scary; they can also be dangerous. Fortunately, as your sobriety days become months and then years, you will experience less and less of these impulses.

When you do experience these urges, does it mean you are doing something wrong, you don't have a good recovery program, and aren't truly committed to sobriety? Of course not. Most likely you're just experiencing memories of the once-important relationship you had with alcohol or other drugs. There are many reminders of your drinking past that still exist in your present and any of these objects, smells, tastes, thoughts, feelings, noises, or people can act as a trigger for some very strong urges.

It's crucial to have the ability to overcome these powerful urges when they spring up. Alcoholics Anonymous refers to this as temporary insanity. How else can you explain the discarding of hard-won months or years of quality sobriety for a few hours of alcohol-induced mental fog? Good intentions aren't enough here and thought power alone will not break the grip of these powerful urges.

The worst thing you can do is to sit and continue to wrestle with the urge. Instead, you need an action plan. This could include physical activity, calling a friend and talking about the urge, or changing your immediate surroundings or current activity. It's best to construct your emergency plan beforehand so that when the urge strikes, you'll know what steps to take.

# CHAPTER 11

# **Relapse Action Plan**

*Three people I can call if I get an urge to drink or use.

1. _____     2. _____

3. _____

*Three activities I can begin which will get my mind off of drinking or using.

1. _____     2. _____

3. _____

When you get the urge to drink or use other drugs, here are the steps you should take:

1.  Call someone on your list. If there's no answer, call the next person on the list. When you reach someone, explain that you are struggling with an urge to drunk or use. Choose one of the activities from your list and tell your friend that instead of using, you're going to do this activity and that when you're finished, you will call again.
2.  Begin an activity from your list. If you can't start any of these, choose something else. What's important is that you

do something—anything but sitting there and thinking about using!

3. After you have finished the activity and the urge has passed, call your friend again and tell that person how you're feeling.

Write your list of support people, phone numbers, and activities on a relapse action-plan card and keep this card in your wallet or purse so it's available when you need it.

**\*\*Recovery Activity**

To make sure your relapse action plan will work when needed, try a practice run. Pretend that you feel like drinking or using other drugs. Now follow through with all three steps of your plan.

# CHAPTER 12

# Building Your Recovery Program

E verything you do to keep yourself sober is your recovery program. Since those who have quality recovery programs stay
sober and avoid relapse, it's a good idea to examine what com-
prises your recovery program. While there are some differences, there
are certain fundamental ingredients that characterize sound and sta-
ble recovery programs.

*Which of the following activities are part of your recovery
program?

_____ Regular and often AA or NA meetings
_____ Daily meditation time/reading of the twelve-step literature
_____ Active practice of the twelve steps
_____ Regular social contact with recovering people
_____ Regular contact with sponsor
_____ Aftercare group
_____ Individual counseling or therapy
_____ Couples or family therapy
_____ Regular journaling
_____ Church or synagogue attendance

# RELAPSE PREVENTION

*The ingredients of my recovery program:

1. _____    2. _____
3. _____    4. _____
5. _____    6. _____
7. _____    8. _____

*Three things I can do to make my recovery program better:

1. _____
2. _____
3. _____

# CHAPTER 13

—ɯ—

# Twelve-Step Groups

G oing to meetings is one of the most important parts of any recovery program. Twelve-step groups will help you work on your sobriety, get support, make friends, and assist others. *Most often, those who attend a regular meeting of AA or NA stay sober, and those who don't relapse.*

Here's a list of qualities to look for in a group:

*Positive Thinking.* A healthy twelve-step group talks positively about recovery. Problems are discussed openly and group members take responsibility for their own actions.

*Common Interests.* You'll probably prefer groups that have interests similar to yours. If group members are quite different from you, it might be difficult to share openly.

*Mutual Sharing.* Meetings where you have a chance to share will help you feel a part of the group. When you feel part of the group, you'll attend regularly and learn about yourself. If you don't share in this meeting, you may feel safe or hidden, but the group won't have much to offer you.

*Available People.* There will be many times you'll need other group members to help you in your recovery. Look for meetings with people you like and can count on for help.

*Recovery Time.* A good meeting will have some members who have been clean and sober for at least a few years. You're going to need support from people who have been around awhile.

\*Meetings I will attend:
Place and time

1. _____
2. _____
3. _____
4. _____

# CHAPTER 14

# Choosing a Sponsor

A sponsor is an AA or NA member who acts as your guide, confidant, and support person. This is the person you can ask for advice or call when you are having a rough day. Choose a sponsor carefully. Your sponsor should be someone who possesses personal attributes you admire—a role model of sorts. Your sponsor should have a few years of sobriety and be the same gender as you so that you feel free to discuss any area of your life.

Name and qualities this person has to offer:

1. _____     _____
2. _____     _____
3. _____     _____

## DEVELOPING SPIRITUALITY

The word spirituality refers to our relationship with a divine principle in the universe. It can also refer to our connection with those groups important to our lives—family, friends, community. It's an appreciation for and an attempt to give meaning to life itself.

Many people starting to recover from the effects of alcohol and other drugs identify a spiritual hunger, a desire for connection with something out there that is greater than themselves and that gives meaning and a sense of direction. Often, this is the starting point for nourishing the spiritual part of their lives. Some people new to recovery have always had strong faiths and now are struggling to reconcile their problems with alcohol or other drugs and their spiritual beliefs.

The first step is recognizing a power greater than yourself—call this power God, the love you feel in your AA meeting, or simply your Higher Power—that you can rely on for help and guidance in your life and in your sobriety.

*What role does a Higher Power play in your life now?

_____

_____

_____

*How can you improve your relationship with your Higher Power:

_____

_____

_____

# CHAPTER 15

# Filling Your Empty Time

D rinking and other drug use take up a lot of time. Whether you were thinking about drinking, using, or recovering from use, most likely it was a major focus in your life. Now you've stopped—what are you doing to fill this empty hole? Simply not using and refusing to make other changes in your life are a recipe for boredom and possible relapse.

*Enjoyable activities which have been neglected:

1. _____    2. _____
3. _____    4. _____

There is a whole world of activities you haven't yet tried. Join a volleyball league, dig a garden, work with wood, volunteer, take evening walks with your partner.

*List new activities you would like to try:

1. _____    2. _____
3. _____    4. _____

# AFTERWORD

—⟋𝔪⟍—

CONGRATULATIONS! You've worked through this entire workbook. You now know what you need to do to keep yourself sober and stay clear of a relapse. You have the tools you need to move confidently into a happy and healthy future recovery.

As both life circumstances and you change, you might find it helpful to rework some of the sections in this guide. Whenever your sobriety feels shaky to you, read through the appropriate section for ideas on how to improve your recovery program and talk with friends, sponsor, and counselor about what you're experiencing. This is the end of the guide, but it is really just the beginning!

**\*\*Recovery Activity**

Put this workbook away and go do something just for you—ride a bike, eat an ice cream sundae, go fishing—anything as long as it's fun!

# ACKNOWLEDGMENTS

T o the men, women, and their families who have allowed me to be a part of their struggle with recovery from the disease of alcohol and drug abuse, you have taught me more about the challenges of this journey than formal education or trainings ever could.

Thank you for sharing your stories and lives with me.

# ABOUT THE AUTHOR

J udy Lohr is a licensed clinical social worker with many years of experience in addictions treatment, Employee Assistance Program counseling, marriage and family therapy, adolescent counseling, and individual and group therapy. Work experience includes being a Beaufort County Drug Court Program director, Beaufort County EAP counselor, marriage and family therapist in Parris Island, Children's Advocacy director, mental health social worker in Beaufort Memorial Hospital, and Beaufort County Alcohol and Drug Abuse Department clinical supervisor. She has a private practice where she still counsels addicts and alcoholics. She currently resides in Beaufort, South Carolina, with her husband Reggie and dog Baxter. They have three grown children and seven grandchildren.

CPSIA information can be obtained
at www.ICGtesting.com
Printed in the USA
LVHW091707290420
654637LV00007B/754